I USED TO BE SOMEBODY

I USED TO BE SOMEBODY

Poetry for Those Up and Over the Hill

THOMAS PLUMMER

ON TARGET PUBLICATIONS
APTOS, CALIFORNIA, USA

ALSO BY THOMAS PLUMMER

I Used to Be Somebody
Poetry for Those Up and Over the Hill

Thomas Plummer

ISBN: 978-1-931046-10-7

Cover photo: Alex Linch, iStock

Acknowledgement is made to the following publishers where these poems first appeared:

"She Was a Mean Beauty"
Beyond Words Literary Magazine, Fall 2022

"God Is Staring at Me"
Beyond Words Literary Magazine, June 2022

"Stolen Love Under a Mountain Moon"
Poets' Choice, Spring 2022

On Target Publications
P. O. Box 1335
Aptos, CA 95001 USA
otpbooks.com

Library of Congress Control Number on file

TO SUSAN

I could have never been me without your love,
your hand, your whisper, your belief in me,
I am me because you never gave up on us.

Old is my only regret.
I need another life of you.
Just another fifty years.
By your side, hand in mine.

I love you... but words never enough.

I imagined you when I imagined love.
I believed in something I never held.

I believed in love I never knew.
This something was always you.

You were the love I always dreamed.

CONTENTS

TODAY

I USED TO BE SOMEBODY

I feel like the old monkey
in the back of his cage at
the zoo. Grayed, wrinkled,
like thousand-year-old parchment,
sitting in my place in the sun,
watching the world pass me
by outside my bars.

Playful youth lost in my
rearview mirror. My once
arrogant swagger now bad
hips and a lean to one side.
Wild nights in the jungle now
dinner at 5:00, asleep by 9:00.

The younger monkeys laugh
and throw banana peels at me.
I scream and howl, *I used to be
like you, I used to be somebody.*

Now I lie on my rock, hoping
the fading rays warm my soul,
sipping something subtle and deep
red. Let young monkeys chase
the nonsense of life, I lie
content, waiting for a warm
bath, a kiss on my saggy jowls.

GOD IS STARING AT ME

Open my eyes, dull dawn light.
Screeching black birds cry outside
my frosted window. Did God send
these reapers of souls after me today?

Not this morning they cackle, but
we know where you live. Glad when
God went to bed, He didn't spit
on my candle.

Do the old man shuffle to the toilet.
Defiantly stare in the mirror. Soon
will be a day my mirror is empty,
the breath of God fogging my view.

Walk the dogs in the wakening
woods. Sun streaking naked out
of its nest. One more day I chant,
just one more, please, yet, would
one day atone for a flawed life
of endless mistakes?

My candle of life burning down,
yet still a defiant flicker, raging
against the coming blackness.
Clouds driven by the wind streak
the sky. Soon, I will be flying
to meet God on their glorious backs.

But not today... my candle still
burns, but God is staring at me,
wetting his fingers...

I WON'T EVEN ANSWER ME

When I talk to myself
I don't usually answer,
but when I do, it's because
I have no idea what the hell
I just asked.... well, myself.

So I tell myself I have no idea
what I just asked myself.
And when I don't even know
what I am talking about,
how can I expect to give
myself a decent answer?

Then I mumble loudly,
you're an idiot old man,
do you even listen to yourself,
which I don't recommend
in the grocery store check-out
line. Poor man, the cashier
whispers. Poor, poor man.

But I don't like to argue, so
I ignore myself, waiting
for me to change the subject.

Rude bastard, do you always
have to be right I snort,
then he just gives me
the silent treatment, all
hurt I called him out.

But I know I am not yet
crazy, because I would have
the decency to tell myself...
if I would only listen.

I AM THE INVISIBLE MAN

I am a comic book
legend, feared by no one,
known by few.

I could rob any shop if it was
run by 20-year-old women.

Some old guy took the money
the cashier mumbles, *they all sort*
of look alike to me. Gray hair, cargo
shorts, white sneakers, you know,
an old guy with no butt.

I walk through a mob of under 30s
at Chick-fil-A, faces down, munching
kale Caesar salads, madly scrolling,
and am never seen... beyond 40 does
not exist in Gen Z world.

I stroll the beaches of Miami,
littered with a 100 lotion soaked
·women, stretched flat in the sand,
strutting the tiniest of bikinis,
yet I am never noticed,
except for the drool.

I stare at a 40s-something woman
in a bar, thick blond hair, wet,
red lips, dressed for a night out
with family. But only her mother
can see me, sadly... so pathetically,
she winks at me.

Even my kids cannot see
me, unless they need money,
then my magic disappears,
revealed by the cash
in my hand.

I am the last of the old
super heroes. I was the king
of the comic book world.
I am the Invisible Man.

MY DAYS ARE TOO FAST FOR ME

Days become nights,
nights lingering longer,
teasing their gift of rebirth.
Morning calling...
come, play, now. Me lost
to the seductiveness
of endless time.

Lost days slowly dance
before me, eyes closed,
seductive black dress,
shimmering lips, there
for my taking, then
fleeing maddingly away
as I reach to embrace her.

I used to keep up
with the days. Savored
their madness, drank
their endless bottle
of life, danced
with each one until
the rising sun. Now,
they are too swift
for me. Once never
ending, now here,
then skittering away.
Fast, faster, another
flees before me.

Wait, please stay,
please slow down.

Dance again...
just for me.

But I am old, slow,
the days too quick.
So many behind me,
you would think they
would treat me with respect,
slowing down just for me,
remembering how much
I loved each one...but so
fast now, too damn fast.

OLD PEOPLE STEW

A six pack of old, naked people
in a hot tub. Boiling stew of wrinkles,
sags, bags, beer bellies, bad hips
and knee replacements.

Glasses hand-painted by Doris
50 years ago, red and yellow peace
signs as flowers, James Taylor crooning
for this bubbling time travel, his CD
picture of torn jeans and long hair,
now bald and soft, one of us at last.
Pass that doobie baby.

Bernie, accountant by day, hipster
by night, rises out of the steam like
a walrus heading to the beach. Paunch,
hairy, white as a bare-ass baby. You
might still have it, Bernie, no one
wants to see it. Oh, brownies,
who made the brownies?

Donna stands naked, passing the smoke.
Breasts once north, now south. Butt once
sassy, still classy, but more of it to love.

Donna? Does anyone now name a kid
Donna, or Doris, Tommy, Bernie, Freddie....
names from the days of Wally and the Beaver.
You still have a bong Freddie?

Raging on... well, at least until 10:00. Creased
khakis, blue work shirts, worn-out rock band
tees scattered on the deck. Naked hippies
roaming the earth. Wet kisses, promises
to get together again soon.

Donna whispers she made fresh
chocolate chippers. Tie-dyed sheets,
a lava lamp, Rod Stewart. A few hours
a month 20 again, not chasing 70.

THE LINE TO HEAVEN

The evil, the mean, the beautiful, the lost.
We shuffle forward, heads down, waiting
our turn, me in this line for decades, time
has no meaning here... but it is hard
to find a toilet in this place.

After a brief touch of eternity, my turn.
God sighed deeply... *so it is you.*
   Did you find the answer to My question?
   Did you get what you wanted from your life?

I raised my eyes to His; a face you give all to see.
   I never knew what I was looking for, but I found it.

   What did you find?

God's face close to my mine,
me, finally touched by the breath
of God... pumpkin spice... yes,
I smell pumpkin spice from Starbucks.

   I was loved by good people. Their
   love enough to heal me. I learned
   to give love. The more I gave, the more
   I received. I found what I wanted, but never
   knew I needed, love enough to save me
   from myself.

He stared at me. Did I travel this far
to be turned away, or sent to the back
of the line... again?

Huge man in a black suit, ear dongle,
sunglasses, waved me to a side door.
   My God, God has bouncers?

God smiled down at me.
Come, there is a glass of wine for you
at your seat at the table…and don't give
Me that look, it is a nice red from Napa.

As I walked ahead, He touched my shoulder.
Love is all I ever asked from you.
I had almost given up, it took so many
years for you to learn such a simple lesson.

MY DAYS AS AN APPLE HEAD

Picked up an apple rolling under foot
at the store. My find once bright red,
heavy, shiny, a specimen admired
by other apples, those lesser
fruits not as voluptuous, but my new
friend bruised and a little lop sided.

The apple reminds me of me. My head
big for my body. Large man, huge,
round head. Looking at my new friend,
I know how Mom felt when I was born.
Giant head baby in her lap, all red
and smooshed.

Both of us have seen better days. If I was
a fruit, I would be banished to the discount
bin... *buy now before he rots* says the sign.
A little mushy, but you can use him for pies.

My old head used to be a good specimen.
Not the best-looking apple on the tree, but
always crisp and sharp. Now, I am this apple,
might be a few good bites in him, but mostly
squishy around the middle.

Hate to throw the little guy away. All us
big, round-headed guys deserve one more
chance. He looked a little beaten on my
counter, but chilled chardonnay and white,
so white cheddar, appeared to save his day.
The proper send-off for a fellow
big-headed friend.

MY GUARDIAN ANGEL IS A DRUNK

One of those hip-flask Baptists, titillating
his lips with a taste of God's own Irish whiskey
between prayers, hiding in the last pew, face
hidden behind a hymn book.

He must be eternally sauced, and the Almighty
surely knows I need Michael himself, the Saturday
night bouncer of angeldom, to keep me walking
between my situational moral lines.

Where was my Flitting Winged Minder when
I ran naked through a country western bar... nothing
on but snakeskin boots, for a five-dollar bet. Probably
line dancing, long neck Bud in hand, stepping it up
with the glowing angel girls of Christmas pasts.

Lose my job, my Whisperer of Sanity ignores me,
off doing shots with strippers at Shotgun Willy's.
I plunge from grace, the smell of heavenly scotch
and cheap beer wisps around my head. Temptation
dances on my crotch, the aroma of earthy wine
whiffs by my nose, his eternal cologne.

He is always there...I hear drunken giggles as I
plunge face in the mud after another disaster
of impurity, my life studied by sinners in Bible
classes, reverends screaming from Sunday pulpits,

> *Look at this man. Be afraid... be afraid.*
> *His life of madness is what you must fear.*
> *He even farted loudly in church, then pointed*
> *to the sweet little lady next to him.*

I was only 13, but I see the holy man's point.

My angel must be a wonder of Heaven. Hovering
close to keep me from dying, my life a continual
stream of *why nots* rather than *no ways*. Sanity
and sensibility... always for you, never me.

I will meet my guardian of life gone bad as we
go arm in arm into eternity. I will buy him
the first 200 shots, thanks for letting me taste
life, love the ones needing love, letting me fall,
always a hidden arm raising me again.

Just for letting me live as me.

WALKING AROUND NAKED IN MY HEAD

My brain, once a well-oiled mechanical
wonder, now a hoarder's attic. Loose wires,
rusted connections, a dusty shoe box of photos,
people we would remember forever no one
remembers.

Over here junk from my wasted youth. Piles
of negativity, hidden under my scratchy blue
blanket of insecurity. And look! A box
of arrogant anger, locked away in a heavy
safe, buried under my pettiness files. My
head now nothing but a cheap yard sale.
Five cents, take all you can carry
and the crap in the dumpster is free.

But wait, my days of light, stuffed in
a yellowed wine box, memories carefully
wrapped I will keep until I am dead... the touch
of my mother's hand on my cheek, holding my
granddaughter for the first time, the bundle I
will be carrying when I bang on the gate
to Heaven.

Oh my, pot from the 70s in a crumpled
baggie under my John Denver cowboy hat,
still smelling like my college girlfriend's hair.
She my first love, once a naked hippie chick
dancing around a campfire... now a principal
in Chicago with three kids and a minivan.

Too much for my withering old brain, I
need to become empty headed, vacuous
as 16-year-old virgins at a prom....
room for remodeling and more tomorrows.

I did keep an old poster. The woman
of legendary curls, living forever in my
teenage dreams, impossible hair begging
to be ruffled, a knowing smile, promising
just enough to make a boy of 16 squirm.

The pot? Yes, I kept the pot.
Old, moving towards pathetic,
but not yet crazy.

ONE MINUTE YOUNG, THE NEXT OLD

Got out of bed to pee. Family
pictures on the wall. Even at night
I can't hide from myself.

Damn photographs, an old man I can't
stand to see... me. My God, saggy cheeks,
a forehead of deep trenches... you could hide
a small child in those. And where is my hair?
Gray patches like an old dog's ass.

They say men age well, but I am now
a scuffed bowling ball, lofted down the lanes
of life too many times by drunken college
students. Wasn't it an hour ago I was young?

Sung *Stayin' Alive* loudly to my fur babies
on the floor. Tried out my 70s dance moves
in front of the mirror.... take that Travolta, no
white suit, but tighty whities and a wrinkled
tee. Please God, let disco come back,
while I still have a little ass to shake.

Crawled back into bed. My wife opened
her eyes. Has she noticed? She went to bed
with a young man, woke with a museum
piece. She touched my face, went back
to sleep. Poor girl, now blind.

I lie in bed, afraid to close my eyes.
I might just wake up dead next time.

NOTHING LEFT TO CHASE

His muzzle a frizzled, motley gray.
White whiskers of morning snow.
Black eyes of infinite wisdom,
he had lived... he had seen it all.

Children call him to play, but he
stays motionless in the sun, head
on outstretched paws. No need
to move, nothing left to chase.

My own world skittering in a haze
of too much of too much, life reduced
to last equations, the unanswerables...
the imponderables of old men. Questions
wrestled by a thousand sages, never
understood by one.

> *Why, why was I here?*
> *Did I matter?*
>
> *Will my eyes open again*
> *on the other side?*

He lays his head on my leg, I stroke
his cheek, slip him a cookie, scratch
scraggily ears.

Everything beautiful dies. Life fleetingly
yours, loaned by a faceless God...
return guaranteed on demand.

In the end, nothing but questions
of worn-out men and quiet sighs
of ancient dogs. Nothing now
but moments in the sun...
just waiting, just wondering.

MY TOMORROW MY YESTERDAY

I closed my eyes for a nap
in my new blue chair, book
in my lap, my kids playing,
my wife young, me with
wavy brown hair.

Phones had cords attached
to the wall, remote controls
were your children, FM late
night rocked baby and Elvis
was still in the building.

So long ago… so, so long.

I mumble and stumble awake.
An hour of drool and wine
induced dreams. My kids
now have kids, my wife a few
decades walk from young. My
brown hair thin wisps of gray
on my scruffy head.

Phones no longer tools
but life itself. The FM late
night jocks of soul long dead.
I yell loudly at a woman
named Siri and she plays quiet
piano music for me.

I still sit in the same chair,
both of us faded and tired...
we will go out together.
I close my eyes and the dreams
still find me. Pictures of what
was, fragments of what I lost,
more time behind than left to me.

So long… so, so long, but
so damn fast when you don't
want it to end. My tomorrows
now my yesterdays.

FORGIVING MYSELF FOR BEING ME

I was born a seeker. I sat in the front pew
singing badly to Jesus. I walked the mountain
trails hand-in-hand with Buddha. I whispered
blessings of the Quran to children. I drank
with the hookers on the streets of New Orleans.

I read Kant and didn't understand a damn word.
Nietzsche just made me want to burn down
the world. I chased saints, sinners, poets
of madness, but not even Ezra could ease my
pain, my search for forgiveness, the only
common word in a 1,000 books on resurrection
of damaged souls. Maybe Hemingway was
right, all paths lead to an old man and a shotgun.

Forgiveness easy to give others. No trespass
too big not to be forgiven. No sin too much
to overcome love, at least that is what I saw
written on the gates of Heaven as I crawled
away, no reservation, try again next year.

Forgiving myself a dance with shadows.
The closed mind of youth died. Nothing
left but the realization we are all perfectly
imperfect. My obsession with perfection
an attempt at walking on water, even
the stone-faced Catholic Jesus on the cross
smiling at that one.

I am you.... you are me, maybe a little beaten,
lost, a life with regret... perfect imperfection,
wonderful messes wrapped in damaged love,
as we were meant to be... and I forgive myself
for being me.

TRUTH OF THE HOURS

Fifth grade, red brick 1930s school.
Ten foot metal-framed windows propped
open with broom handles. Early May, hot sun,
summer calling dreary children. Two o'clock
the big black hands of the wall clock says,
the screaming horde set free at 3:00...
that hour a year of my life.

College, 19, case of beer, my hippie van,
my first love riding shotgun. Heading
to a cheap motel near the lake, an hour
from our dorm rooms. The promise
of love so near, a frustrating ride
of anticipation, the only hour of my life
I needed a calendar to track the months.

Standing by a window 12 floors up,
staring out at everything, and nothing,
my mother of 79 quiet in front of the desk...
waiting for her doctor to return. Stay here
he said, but it could take an hour. I thought
my watch stopped, shook it hard, every
minute of the hour an hour. Time
changed nothing, nothing more we can
do he said, take her home, make her
comfortable, not much time left.

I sit now with my wife. I hold her hand
as we read.... as I have done for decades.
I glance at my phone, has it been an hour?
Minutes now seconds, years now hours.
Ten years ago yesterday. Time fleeing
over the mountains like terrified deer.

I cling to time now, sometimes late night
tears remembering what was, wishing endless
hours for the one I love, knowing the truth
of the hours, knowing there is one final one
waiting for me.

YESTERDAY

SLOW DOWN, YOU WILL KILL US ALL

Slow down you old fool, you're driving 55,
you are going to get us murdered on this road...
murdered damn you.

I was 10, in the back seat behind my unperturbed
grandfather, alongside my grandmother of 75, a good
Catholic girl not afraid of a swear word, or glass of wine...
I need to pee, I hate to get murdered with pee pee pants.

You damn idiot, can't you see that truck.
My hand on the door handle, ready to jump
rather than be crushed in a lime green Ford Pinto,
drenched in my own urine, nothing left of me
but soiled underpants.

She screamed in Papa's ear, but at 80 I didn't
know if he couldn't hear or if he mastered
ignoring her, humming a farm song from his
youth. Maybe WW I prepared him for her.
Machine guns and rattling tanks had nothing
on a mean-ass farm girl who birthed nine kids.

He drove, she in the backseat, told she was safer
there. My father once gave him a chauffer's hat
she snatched off his head and slapped him with it.

We arrived home, not mangled, Grandpa nodding
to my dad, the knowing man walking toward the firing
squad, at peace with death, or a long life with a 100-
pound gray-haired tornado. She slammed the door,
the fool, the man cannot drive, I will die in that car;
he will kill us all.

Grandpa died two years later. The 15-year-old car
sitting in their dirt-floored garage, covered in dust and bird
crap, left to rust until Grandma passed three years beyond.

Seven thousand miles, sold cheap to a high school kid,
the grandkids terrified of driving it, knowing an eternally
distressed ghost would be shrieking over their shoulders,
*slow down, you will kill us all, you're driving too damn fast
you young fool.*

WET LEAVES

Wet leaves, a childhood memory
when I was 17... buzz cut,
cheap jeans, big white cuffs, almost
a man, still so much a child.

Mom, barely five feet, me already
looking down at her. My stepfather, out
a month, picking up a last cardboard
box, but time to give her one last slap
and shove against the wall.

She leaned against my chest, tears, her
cheek a throbbing purple, silent. His 10-
year reign of terror over, a last reminder
why I prayed daily for his death.

Mom popped a beer and sat at the table, go,
go to the game, I will be fine, he's gone.
I kissed her cheek, took her keys, left.

A wet fall... black, pungent leaves blowing
down our street, breathing the promise of an ugly
winter. A boy of anger, wanting to smash his face,
knowing he knocked me down more times
than I could remember, a practiced drunk,
happy in barfights, but only if they were not
much bigger than my mom.

I kicked through leaves, pounding my fists
on the hood of the car. One kick... a roll of money
flying, tightly crunched in a blue rubber band.
$400 in 20s. I swept floors in a store
that summer for a $1.75 an hour.

I handed the wad to Mom. She peeled off $20
for me, hid the rest under the sink. Small payment
for the pain, but I hadn't seen her laugh in years.

I moved the car to the church parking lot up
the street, crying, knowing he would be back.
The preacher and son cutting grass. Can I hide
the car behind the church? He nodded, I ran
back home. We hid behind closed curtains,
doors locked, locks changed, Mom's hand
near the phone, waiting to call the police,
regulars at our house that year.

He was back in 10 minutes, kicking leaves
where he parked, angrier by the kick. Nothing,
gone, lost. He stared at the house, taking steps
forward.

The preacher and son wandered down
the street, sat on our steps, reading Bibles
as if it was just another day visiting God,
wedged between an angry drunk and a terrified
woman. He waved his fist at them, screamed curses...
and nothing... they smiled, nodded, prayed.

The old man slammed his door, screeching
tires up the street in his dented Mercury cruiser.
The preacher wrapped ice in a dish cloth, pressing
it against her cheek, his son standing guard
on the porch. I sat all afternoon staring out
the window, waiting, hand on the phone.

I still smell the dead leaves...
still feel the fear.

WHY DOESN'T HE LOVE US?

46... 47... 48... 49... 50, silver, red, blue, every car but his.

Told you, he is not coming. Come on little brother, give it up.

He said he will be here at 10:00.

It's 11:00.

Call him again.

*I just called him, you watched me call him,
he didn't answer, he won't answer.*

Let's count another 50 cars, he will be here, I know it.

He is not coming, stop crying, he doesn't care.

*You heard him, he promised, he swore to us,
he swore he would be here this time.*

I am going to ride my bike, we are wasting Sunday.

Sitting on our sagging bed, staring out the alley
window. We see cars passing at the end of the road.
Magically appearing out of the side of Elmer's little
store,
disappearing in front of the New Moon bar. Left to right,
left to right, the way he would come... if he came.

I am staying here, he will be here, I know he will be here.

He lied to us again, he lied to us last Sunday,

he doesn't care anymore. Come with me?

Go ahead, I am going to hang here.

I ruffled my brother's hair, left him alone.

*1... 2... 3... 4... 5. Come on Dad, please,
please show up this time.*

67

Had a beer with my dad the other day...
a few times a year I open a can
of the cheap stuff, his once-daily favorite.
He would die again if he knew Pabst
was now a hipster beer. Skinny jeans
and scraggily beards drinking tallboys
on a Friday afternoon, paying more
for the can than he did a case.

He is me and I am him, but I never
knew him. He ran away when I was six,
under the spell of a long-legged blonde
who wanted nothing to do with his kids.

The 15 minutes between our houses
could have been 5,000 miles of desert.
We were embarrassingly poor, banned
from their house when I was 13,
too wild, too messy, just too his...
but also someone else's.

Saw him again when I left for college.
We were at least talking. He handed me
a check for $67 and laughed,
  When this runs out get a job.

I'm his oldest son, but didn't know him.
My brother there his last years. Dad
a ghost to me before he was a memory.
We loved him because he was our father...
we hated him because he wouldn't be.

I visit his grave once a year, a cold moss-
covered stone covering a cold man.
Why couldn't you see us? Love us?
Why this cheap beer, you crazy,
old man... and 67, why 67?

LEAVING NOWHERE FOR ANYWHERE

Four little churches built on hope of rescuing
the hopeless, but they still couldn't save my soul.
Wasn't a day passed I didn't think of beating
my stepfather to death with his own beer bottle.
Drunks pissing on the church walls at 3:00 in
the morning, passing out on steps leading
to a God they couldn't find.

We lived where white trash found cheap rent.
Factories shuttered, stripped by scavengers,
even the windows stolen.... yet, no one left.
Easier to sit in a bar at 7:00 in the morning,
shooting cheap whiskey, collecting the welfare,
than admitting the minute you open your eyes
you are too drunk to ever work again.

Went to school in the next town. Pretty little homes
with fences and swings, fathers who didn't smack
their kids after a few beers. Started as the worst
dressed kid... torn, worn-out jeans, yellowing tee
shirts, scuffed work boots from my grandfather.

Only took a few months to see my way out.
What I could learn could be who I became.
Worked hard, was beaten hard, yet he couldn't
smack the hope out of me.

Bought decent pants from throwing bales
for local farmers, even wore a new blue shirt.
Left when I was 18. Gave the rear view mirror
the finger as I drove past the edge of town.

Our three-room nightmare still standing. Forced
myself to see it with my brother on a hot summer
day. He cried when we turned onto the street. Smaller
than we remembered. Empty, dreary, I still feel
the hate. We drank beer on the porch. Talked about
buying it to burn it down.

Someone once asked me where I am from. Nowhere
I said. You have to be from somewhere he laughed.
I am here… that is enough.

HE WHO WAS ME

Who I was, I am no more.
Older now, but another.
Who I was, gone.
Who I will be, not yet born.

The mistakes of he, who was me,
don't matter to me, that was him.
That me died years ago. All he left
me was me, but me is enough. But
how could he, so young, know the he
who was then was so wrong?

I am now me, but still surprised
by this me. Finally, I am the other one
I hoped to be. If I live long enough,
I will become him, no longer me, but
who he was, I was, so long ago when
who I was mattered.

I forgive him, the one who was me,
because without him I wouldn't be me.
yet, I am glad he was me and now
is not me… he was a crazy bastard…
I am glad he is gone.

MY LAST GOODBYE

I still remember. My mother standing in her driveway waving goodbye. Five feet tall, maybe a hundred pounds... frail, the end of days chasing her hard. Her wispy, silver-streaked hair blowing in the hot afternoon winds on the hill where she lived. Thought she might blow into the clouds in a big gust. I waved and drove away as she threw me a kiss, but I didn't make it a mile. I pulled over crying, trying to pull myself together enough to drive to the airport. Another short visit as I crisscrossed the country doing my work. In for a day... out again. I called her again on my way, "What did you forget?" she laughed. "Uh, maybe a shirt Mom, I think I left a shirt in the closet. I'll get it next trip... I love you Mom, call you when I get home." Never held her again, never felt her hand on my cheek. Why didn't I stay, just one more day, just one more hour?

BAD DAY TO BE GRANDPA

Every doorknob painted green.
Watch her, my daughter says...
just for a few hours.
A nap, okay, I fell asleep in my chair.
Granddaughter naked in the utility sink.
Me scrubbing paint off her face
Well, hello honey, home early?

FIRST DATE

The more you drink,
the better I look....
so let me pour you
another glass, my love,
I am still a few sips
shy of handsome.

THE END OF MY BEGINNING

My future is my end.
My end, my beginning.
The beginning where I start again,
reborn into my own life.
Living once more.
Chasing an end that never ends.
Always just new beginnings.

SO MANY DAYS TO DIE

Another year gone.
Each day passes
on my calendar.
Wondering... 365 choices,
which will be the day I die?
My day first remembered
by a few who loved me.
Then, weeks, months,
years pass them by,
my day forgotten...
as they will be too.
This remembrance
taken by others who
trade back the day
of their birth
for the day
of their death.
I hope my day is
the first of the month.
Make it a Monday.
Easy to remember...
and I hate to waste
a weekend.

STOLEN LOVE UNDER A MOUNTAIN MOON

Rocky Mountains high
plateau. Wine, warm
blankets, stolen love
at midnight.

A love that should have
never been. The full
moon near enough
to burn my soul.
Dew on the meadow
grass, crisp chill
in the late August air.

Alone as you can ever
be in this world, nothing
but elk and the sounds
of night for miles.

Two people hiding.
Hours spent loving
in the dark, love
that could never be
in the light of day.

Running naked
under the moonlight.
Dancing in open
meadows of wet grass,
glimmering piles of snow
under the bushes,
Love, freedom, stars
we reached to touch.

Summer love
not mattering
to either of us.

Lost in lust
and youth.
Escaping lives
neither wanted.

Finding beauty
in the stillness.
Free to run wild
in the brilliant light,
light not felt by those
who never seek
the high meadows.

We loved until the sun
broke through the morning
mist, a night without time.
Demanding love we
never found in others.
Letting her love save me.
She dancing forever
in my mind, both of us
forever young,
hidden nights
at the top
of the world.

POETS OF THE MIDNIGHT HOUR

I thought living dead would rule
the world, now I believe hordes
of poets will outlive the cockroach,
stalking the nights, forever shouting
verses to the shadows of darkness,
sitting up in the wee hours debating
personal madness shared in a poem.

Every frustrated retiree a secret poet,
sleeping with a notebook and beautiful
pen, waiting for the late-night rush
of hidden secrets to fill the pages,
drooling cold coffee, writing
just one more line.

Every struggling artist a romantic
poet, every failing musician writing
poetry in a song no one sings,
desperately scribbling, the last act
of defiance, searching for magic
lines to change his fortune.

The wonder of poetry is you can write
so badly the humbled readers think you
are good. I don't understand a word,
it must be brilliant. You write to bare
your soul and set your demons free,
but I am not sure I want to see you naked
the reader mumbles.

Your words of misery turn into books
of poetic pain, leaving me needing
a happy puppy poem, many glasses
of soothing wine, all to purge the pain
you inspired.

We writers of coffee shop poetry
are a strange breed of poetic insanity.
We take the worst moments of life
and celebrate it in four verses.
No one we have devastated or slept
with safe from a midnight poem.

The harder we crash, the more tears
per line. Nothing to write? Kick out
the love of your life and now you have
a true work of the painful art. Dredge
up family secrets and you will make
that deadline. Tell the scandalous
and poetry flows like honey.

And what poet doesn't hate loving
parents and a functional family?
The writing life is difficult surrounded
by normal people, people who love you
unconditionally, never satisfying your
darkest need for more drama per word.

We are all poets of the damaged soul.
We all seek lines to change the world.
We have no choice but to create our
verses of personal love and pain.
We are all poets of the midnight
hour, and I love you all.

TOO CLOSE TO THE EDGE

San Francisco my lost years. Work
I hated... women who hated me,
a master of barely surviving.

A troubled man lived in bushes behind
my office. Larry, six feet, scraggly,
greasy silver hair, the smile of a child.

Reality and Larry had parted ways.
Red-green, green-red, green-red,
money dirty, you got pretty clothes,
his usual greeting as he wandered lower
Fillmore, too gone to ask for change.

I took care of him, cops ignored him,
leaving him to live or die on the streets.
Bought him clothes and snuck him in for
a shower when the boss was gone, burning
his street clothes, cutting his filthy hair.

He waited for me to close, popping out
of the bushes to walk me toward my tiny
apartment, a shabby place underground
not much nicer than his bush. He never talked,
but knew my name, shuffling along, waiting.
I handed him cash I could spare... maybe
extra dollars stolen from the register.

He would head to the liquor store, coming out
with a bottle, smokes, and if I gave him enough,
a sandwich. After a bitter day mucking up my job,
I followed him into the store for my own bottle.

We sat against the wall, watching pretty party
people drift into trendy night spots. Two drunks,
sipping and staring, one crazy, the other close
behind, dancing too close to the edge.

I looked at Larry's face, wondering
if he knew when he lost it, wondering
if I will know when I cross that line?
Red-green, green-red, green-red,
money dirty, you got pretty clothes...
                    it makes sense to me.

A LOVE THAT ALMOST KILLED ME

She stole my checkbook, drained my last
dollar, wrecked my car drunk on a Saturday
afternoon. Left me waiting at bars, staring
at the door, wondering if she would show.
Lost her cat... cried in my arms. I bought
her a new one ... she gave the damn
thing away the next day.

Slept with my ex-best friend, shrugged
as if I would understand. Lost a job
because she was endlessly late, got it
back with promises she would never keep.
Wore high heels as tickets to free drinks.
Lived with me when she needed me,
lived alone when she didn't.

Loved strip bars, lap dances, the gay bars
of San Francisco. Always one shot away
from on stage... I bought her that shot.

Broke up with me at noon, knocked
on my door at 3:00 a.m. dragging
her suitcase. One shake of that copper
hair and I forgave her everything...
might have even been my fault.

Hurt me enough to make me want
to be a monk alone in a cave. So wild
woman in bed I was glad I wasn't.

Left one day and I never saw her again.
One year, three months, six days
of loving her. You get old, you forget
the pain, but cling to the heat.

YOUR UNDERWEAR IS OLDER THAN SHE IS

You are 64. Your daughter is
older than she is. Your underwear
is older than she is.

Hadn't seen him in four years.
Grew up three houses apart, poor
as senseless drunks, which our
fathers were.

We left town, made money, but still
idiots who grew up stealing cases
of beer from delivery trucks. He married,
then married, then married again, and now...
searching again for true love. All he found
so far was eternal alimony.

Why not get manscaped... wear tight, white
tee shirts? So cliché to date the nanny. And tan,
why are you so tan? You smell funny, is that body
spray? You stink like a fermented teenager.

She is my yoga instructor. We live
together. Be nice, here she comes...
six feet, black hair, blue eyes, red lips,
matching dress, yoga had been good
to her. She kissed me on the cheek.
I have heard so much about you.

Checked my phone as I left, a picture
of us just taken. Same age, me a 100
years older, nights of reading, soft music,
early in bed, happily lost in the quiet
routines of the newly old.

I glanced at them. My God that would
be work. Here honey, I will play some
music. Never heard of Rod Stewart?
How about some Van Morrison?
And sex??? I hope his heart is strong,
but if he dies in bed he will be a legend.

But love? She held his hand with both
of hers, leaning in to kiss him, a lonely
man still chasing the dream.

WANDERING ALONE IN THE DARK

Threw away an old friend, a folding clock,
silver finish, big numbers, engraved cover
folding down into its stand at night. Always
the pale glow of moonlight.

A friend dead many years gave me the clock
on a birthday long ago. Here, you always
oversleep... I brought it from Europe,
it will last longer than we will.

It sat on the top shelf of my writing desk,
a reminder of my days as a road warrior.
Now, nothing but a taunt of books never finished,
cities not walked, mountain air never breathed,
nothing left but daydreams of an old man.

The clock's song at first a comfort on dark nights
writing alone. Always there, seldom noticed, part
of the rhythm of my work.

Finally, I closed it, its message too personal,
too close to my fading reality. Tick, tick, tick...
minutes, hours, days, time relentlessly running
ahead of me, its time endless... mine not.

Took my old friend off its perch, wrapped it
in soft cloth, drove to the mountains, blue
evening haze calling me. Hiked to the top
of a waterfall, the place where time stops
for me. Climbed down to where water
crashed into ancient rock, buried the clock
under a heavy boulder.

Gesture of a man slipping his mind, an act
of defiance in a fight I am losing. Watched
the water fall until dark. Wasting time, wasting
the hours, the last one off the trail. Wandering
alone in the coming darkness.

I STILL WHISPER YOUR NAME

Alone in a crowded cemetery, me
and a field of ghosts, all wondering
why no one visits. North wind whisking
dead flowers at my feet. Nothing
to stare at but your name on a stone.

Your friends who are left no longer sing your
name, your place at the table forgotten. We buried
you shoulder to shoulder, vowing to remember,
but passing years the cruelest of thieves, leaving
nothing but fleeting images of one who was you.

Long years, endless hours, you built a fortune.
Your money now gone, your dreams buried with you.
Your wife married to one not a cold remembrance.
The man of business, of wealth, who could not be
replaced you said, dying on your office floor at 52.

But you have me my friend. You are not forgotten.
I still sing your song, still sit on this stone bench,
my gift to you, remembering... just remembering,
whispering your name.

NO REASON FOR TOMORROW

His wife dead three years, buried
on a frigid February morning, along
with what was left of his life.

He found a home in a local bar. Stool
near the television. Four o'clock every day.
Three glasses of draft beer. Enough to let
him forget. Old guys sharing yesterdays.
Watching games on Saturday.

The owner died, the bar closed, he had
nothing left. His wife had been his life.
No friends but her. Days and nights
for 50 years, laughs and loves, kids
and dreams. Then... gone.

He sits on the edge of their bed. Same
frilly pillows. Her glasses and unfinished
book on the nightstand. Him believing
she is just in another room.

Find a reason to live his kids scream.
Make friends. Leave the damn house,
Dad. Find a reason to get up tomorrow.

He crawls into bed, the light on,
as always, on her side of the bed.

Closes his eyes,
praying for sleep,
praying to forget,
praying he never will.

His hand on her pillow.
Goodnight love, sleep well.

THE POINT OF NO RETURN

He sat drinking alone. Quiet,
but polite, no interest in the women
drifting in through the long evenings.

He left early, leaving a nice tip
for the woman who ran the place.
Thank you, see you tomorrow.
He smiled, a wave of goodbye.

His road home ran under a train bridge.
Enormous pillars of concrete pushing it
high above the highway.

They say he was doing a 130 when his
car hit the wall, no signs of braking, full
on until impact. They buried what
was left of his car; he now one with
the machine that killed him.

Years later, I drove past his wall late at night,
pulled up with my lights on the faint imprint.
I was in shadow times, trapped by self-inflicted
pain, wondering when I stopped feeling, when I
quit caring.

What were his last thoughts as he punched down
the peddle, committing to a fiery death a mile
up the road? Was he smiling at the relief?

Left a beer against the wall, remembrance to one
who found death easier than another lonely night
at the end of the bar. Drove home slowly, mumbling
prayers of forgiveness for his damaged soul,
another for my own. Fleeting glimpses of peace
he found I have never known.

Please keep me from the wall.
Please help me find my way home.

TOMORROW

YOU WILL SURVIVE THE DARKNESS

You crash to the bottom,
wondering if you
can live another day.
Waves of pain relentlessly
wash over you, leaving you
praying, begging your suffering
ends, so you can breathe again,
so your crying stops.

The pain will end. Misery fades,
you look back, startled you survived,
the worst the universe used to destroy
you not enough to kill your soul.

You crawl out the other side
of hopelessness, clawed raw
by the terror of your nights,
reborn, tempered by the beating,
full of rage, defiant in the light,
arms raised, screaming to the sky,
not today, not to me, never again
will I be weak.

You rise from the shadows, life
beginning again. You find a still
peace letting you rest, discovering
indestructible strength in your
torn heart, courage you now
know can be yours.

Then you live.
then, and only then,
you become
who you were
meant to be.

TOO BUSY FOR LOVE

A touch of early spring sends
me to the park, weak sun warming
my pale face. I watch a young
father across the path, making love
to his phone, two little girls kicking
a ball in the new grass. Spring dresses,
pink jackets and rubber boots covered
in brightly painted flowers.

The girls break into *Five Little Monkeys
Jumping on a Bed* and I sing along
to myself. The father, earbuds in,
furiously pounding, talking loudly,
gestures of frustration only I can see.

One sits quietly next to him taking his
arm. She smiles up at him. She waits.
She should have sent him a text.

She slides down still smiling, but they
never forget. He is Dad, he is perfect…
until the day he isn't.

I want to tell him how it will end. I want
to scream love for a child is simple… be
present when love appears, and the love
of a child will be yours forever.

They leave, girls holding hands,
father trailing behind, still in love with his
phone, a man who doesn't know what
he just lost.

WAIT? WHAT KIDS?

Their heads are dead I said.
Poor babies, too much phone.
Eyes glassy, lips sassy, butts gassy.
Necks bent like old flamingos.
So young, looking so damn old.
Imagination murdered by the hour.
Turn it off please, you can't breathe.
No they scream, my phone is life.
Bedroom lights on at 2:00 a.m.
Tap, tap, tap, their little fingers fly.
Earbuds glued to tiny ears.
Too young we moan, you are too young.
But all my friends have one they cry.
Nothing but tops of heads.
Sit, stare, drool, peck, sit, stare.
Sound asleep, phone on chest.
Some kid babbling on the other end.
Try a book I beg granddaughter?
Yucky, icky, how do you make it talk?
Texts from the living room, drink please.
My God, child, rise from the couch.
Bean bag babies now our kids.
Soft, mushy, mushrooms of lost youth.
Walk, at least walk dammit.
Wait, can I bring my phone?
The seductive glow of crack pings.
The devil's smile in warm blue light.
Pavlov's dogs never were as fast.
Doesn't matter who it is.
Now, now, I must answer now.
Parents, parents please save us all.
Wait, what, I was on my phone?
What kids? I have kids?

WINE, I LOVE YOU

A week of a thousand days. Eating
stress like a junkyard dog, sprawled
in dirt chewing on a smelly boot.
Four o'clock arrives, I am blessed
by the redemptive powers of wine.

Wine is God speaking to us. One glass,
a soothing balm, One sniff, proof Heaven
is a vineyard. Light dancing on my
glass, divine intervention, the face
of God in the swirling reds.

I sip, I think, I melt, I sigh. Pain
around my eyes fades, strain
in my voice eases. Two glasses...
I am giggly, and maybe see my
wife's come-hither smile as she
peeks over her book.

Wine, a celebration of long-dead kings,
a touch of the divine power of ancient
Romans. Hidden, stained casks, midnight
smiles of monks sipping and praying
the night away. Even Jesus raised a glass
of thanks at dinner with a few friends.

And why I drop to a knee and bow,
acknowledging the humble clerk
at the wine shop, my source
of earthly salvation.

My glass in hand a tribute.
The full bottle a sign,
a celebration of the bounty
of a God who loves me.

DOING THE UNDERWEAR BOOGIE

Come on y'all, dance along,
we're doing the underwear
boogie.

Dance, man, dance.
Bare ass naked
in front of the mirror.
Bend... slowly bend down,
creaks, moans, whimpering,
a-thousand voice choir
of complaints; knees, back,
hips, a chorus of
"You have to be
kidding, old man."

Come on y'all, we're doing
the underwear boogie.

Left leg hole up over left foot.
Boogie to the right
on the other leg.
Hop, hop, hop, almost got it.
Hang on to the top
with both hands.
Dance back to the right
on the other.
Hop, hop, hop,
3-2-1... pull quickly.

Come on y'all, we're doing
the underwear boogie.

Stand all proud.
Underwear hanging
on the thighs.
Bend slowwwwlly
down again.

Lift high… hiiiiigherrrrr!!!
Dance old man, dance.
Hop, hop, hop, hop…
Circle to the left,
circle to the right.

Come on y'all, we're doing
the underwear boogie.

Jump high, pull hard,
underwear now up.
Hands on the hips.
Head back.
Glare at the me
in the mirror
Stare that fool down.
Victory mine.
Arms high in salute.
The daily underwear
war won.

Oh, crap…
inside out.

ALWAYS IN MY DREAMS

Rain moving in hard. Me hiding
by the fire, head back in my worn
chair, watching the rain line moving
closer, driven by the coming storm.

Close my eyes and she is there.
90s rock star auburn hair. Short, black
leather skirt. Spiky, red heels. Standing
near me in a circle of friends. Cocktails,
throbbing music, a few shots setting
the hormones on fire.

The music slows, lights dim, she is
in my arms. Dancing a clinging
embrace to *Kiss from a Rose*, just
us, alone in a crowd of a hundred.
We shuffle to the door, her hand
in mine, walking to our hotel,
hands swinging slowly.

She steps under my arm, head
on my shoulder, our first kiss,
a hint of expectation, wanting
more, still shy with each other...

> 30 years, I never
> let go of her hand.

She slides into her chair, the storm
moving closer, hair still red... we
still dance, mostly in the living
room these days.

Has it been 30 years, I ask?

Yes, honey.

Glad we danced.

Glad you asked me.

I miss that leather skirt.

You are a disgusting, old man.

And the heels, I miss the heels.

*Well.. I might have those in
the trunk, we can look
for them later.*

MY SUNDAY AFTERNOON NAP

Go away world, you are bothering me...
dark, rainy day and you so bore me.
A nap... time for a nap.

The heavy quilt, a friend I've known
longer than my wife. A thousand fragments
making one blanket... mismatched flowers,
farmhouses, meadow scenes, swatches
of barn red, faded golds, royal blues,
no pattern, colors from a century gone,
yet all fit together creating something
still alive after 80 years.

My grandma, and an organized army
of day-sipping wine drinkers, hand
sewed this cloth Picasso 10 years
before my birth. Stories told, lives
shared, sip and sew, sip and sew.

Tried to be productive today.
Up early, walked the cloudy roads
before the first drizzle. Early afternoon
and we turn on the lights. Pounding rain,
temperature dropping 15 degrees. Floors
so cold I dig out my furry slippers. Winter
called ahead... I am coming soon.

We pile onto the bed, buried under
the quilt. Two Boston Terriers snuggled
behind. Wife on the other side, cuddling
in to get warm. Rain blowing against
the windows. Rivulets driven up
the glass by the north wind. Dogs,
hidden and snoring, wife breathing
soft rasps of sleep, branches
snap, snap against the glass.

Let it rain, let it dance,
let it sing until it dies. Get up
and write about this. I should
get up and make notes, I should…

WHERE YOU GO, I GO

Waited behind bushes on the corner.
Followed you home from school.
We were nine. Took me a month
to ask to carry your books.

Where you went, I wanted to go.

You left for college in Michigan.
Me to Illinois. Didn't last
three months. Quit, packed, drove
all weekend. Finished school living
together in a shabby apartment.

Where you went, I had to go.

Painted your new law office.
Celebrated your first win. Two
careers, three kids, married
42 years. Retired. Grandkids.
Beaches. Travel. Grew old.
Every picture by your side.

Where you go, I go.

The single love of my long life.
Pinging of the monitor. You
always a fighter, but a fight we
can't win. Nurse's touch on my
shoulder. Your hand, finally,
letting go of mine. Slept alone
for the first time in 50 years.

The kids visit. Grandkids call.
I sit in my chair late at night.
Quiet, waiting for your voice.
Old, tired, spent, alone.

Soon my love, soon.
Where you go, I must go.

EVERYBODY USED TO BE SOMEBODY

The only thing alive in this
cemetery is light dancing on
the top of gleaning marble.
Stone plaque on the gate...
established 1878. Who was
customer one, did he get
a special introductory rate?
First in, best deal for you
my friend.

Gentle slopes, glistening pond
bubbling at the bottom of the hill,
the first residents nearest the water,
everyone has a good view
of the mountains.

Rows upon rows of lost dreams,
failed marriages, big mortgages,
troubled children... and the belief
death happens to anyone but me.

Everybody here used to be somebody,
people believing the world couldn't
live without them, now spending
eternity proving themselves wrong.

Death fades us into gray canvas,
our color stolen by relentless years.
A loving mother lies here, now nothing
but a black and white cracked picture
in a shoe box... my mother's mother
someone mumbles, who vaguely
smelled like lavender.

The sergeant here served in Korea,
now 50 years later no one stops
to remember, the ones who would
never forget now long gone, dead
flowers blown from other graves
piled against his stone.

Here is Sarah Jane, born 1921...
died 1934. Long dead before
she began. Grieving parents
who swore to cling to her soul,
yet here she is, alone, nothing
but a weathered, faded stone
on a hot summer day. Is she
yet a memory in the head
of anyone still alive?

Five years after we're dead
no one gives a damn. Here we
are, there we go, fading away
one lost memory at a time,
one generation from forgotten.

But here, here is one to
remember, at least until
I claim my spot alongside
the others here.

Joseph Cotton, lived to 88,
a simple inscription on his stone...
I didn't know she was married

AT LEAST I REMEMBERED I FORGOT

I can't remember what I can't
remember, but I was supposed
to do it today... or maybe yesterday.
At least I remembered I forgot.

It used to be on the tip of my tongue.
Now, I hope it is at least clinging
to my old ass. I remembered to remember,
but all I remembered is I have no idea
what I remembered I forgot.

My friends are the same. Remember
that guy, we cackle. Ah yeah, the one
guy from that one trip, yeah I remember
him. Short guy, big ears, talked loudly.
We all nod, yeah that's him... none of us
a damn clue who we are talking about.

I once recited poetry over dinner. Now,
can't remember the author's name. I sit
at midnight looking up my favorites again.
Hey, these are good, I am glad I forgot
so I can remember again.

I read poems of lost love, tears in my
eyes for a woman I once loved, but
no longer know her face. I remember
the longing, but little of the woman.

We forget so much because we
knew so much. Old heads like junked
up drawers... my underwear in there
somewhere, I just have
to keep digging.

I remember I forgot, I forgot
to remember. I remember again...
days after I lost it all, but there it is,
all I forgot to remember when I
remembered what I forgot.

TEN MILES EAST OF HEAVEN

Please God, hear my prayer.

I stand lost Lord, 10 miles east
of Heaven, searching for the gate
many long years. Confused, lonely,
sitting alongside this road, waiting
for the merciful universe
to show me the way.

I wandered this earth chased
by fire. Wondering who
I am, what am I doing here?
The burden I carry pale
compared to others, those
suffering the infinitely
unimaginable, taken by flames
of death, loss, failure, addiction.
I am a man blessed, yet
weakened in spirit, worn
down by my 70-year walk.

I stand weary at this crossroad,
staring down roads I must
yet walk, hoping for the hand
of a silent God, committing
to Your road and a home I
have never touched,
but drawing me onward.

I want to have mattered.
I want to be remembered
as a man who gave life.
I want to go where the pain
is no longer mine.

I am ready Lord, I am ready
to find my way home.

SAYING GOODBYE TO MYSELF

I was the worst of lovers to myself. What
my testosterone-crazed mind conceived,
my young, indestructible self believed.
My body now a 100 miles of dirt road
beyond young, every inch damaged
by potholes of stupidity, toxic mud,
sharp rocks of ego, more road kill
than road hero.

This ship wreck of a body sings to me
like a petulant four-year-old, irritating songs
of pain and misery, reminding me we both
used to be somebody. There is talk, a rumor
I hope, you might even want to leave me soon.

Never respected you in my younger days. We
never slept because the party never ended, too
much of the wine, midnight song, the women,
my God me, we chased the women.

Why take care of you then…we were immortal,
the two of us invincible as others aged, but not us.
Totter off to bed old people, turn down that last glass,
be pathetic, never happen to us we laughed.

Then you betrayed me. My mind young,
my body declaring a war of total attrition,
a battle to the death between my man-child
brain, and my body's dedication to punishing
me for past sins.

Soon old buddy, you will need to go
on your way, alone, leaving me behind.
I will miss you friend, but I must continue
my journey without you. Places I need to be.
Seeking my place…beyond the pain.

NOTHING IS MINE

Read until I couldn't read, maybe
1:00 in the morning. Closed my book,
turned out the light, sat in the dark
watching moon shadows dancing
in the bare trees in my woods.

I have everything... and have nothing.
We pass through life as if we were
playful shafts of moonlight,
touching everything, never able
to hold on to any of it. We embrace
all we touch, wrapping light around
all we encounter, believing we own
what we can never own.

Our words of love as fleeting as
a spring flower... days, years,
a lifetime, it doesn't matter, here,
blooming, gone by the hands
of harsh winters demanding all
must die to be reborn.

All mere moments of fleeting
moonlight, my daughter's laugh,
a puppy cuddled in my lap,
an "I love you" from the grandchild,
even the burning touch of my wife's
hand as she strokes my old face,
mine... my light, until none of it
is mine anymore.

We all die alone, surrounded
by those we love, none of them
coming with us. Just you, death
a final reminder nothing really
matters, nothing really yours,
all just touches of your light.

YOU ARE NOT ALONE

You are not alone. I don't
know the battles you fought,
the beatings you have taken.
I regret the stealing
of your years of innocence.
But I will listen....

Take my hand... let us sit
quietly, I will hear your stor
of pain, I will not let you
go through this alone.

I will tell you shattered dreams
shape your life. I will whisper
I am here, he is gone,
you are safe with me,
your head on my shoulder,
your time for tears.

The numbing fear in your eyes
fades. The flinch at a door opening
in the night stops. The terror of heavy
footsteps and the rattle of whiskey
bottles ends.

Your crying is your healing,
Your pain of a thousand days
of fear is over... your time now
to live again.

Take my hand... let me lift you.
Hear my words, let the healing
begin. Sit by my side and know
I am here for you.

You, beaten but never submitting,
damaged, but stronger, tempered
by a fight only you could win.

I can, and will,
stand by my friend.
Take my hand, you
are not alone.

THE BEAUTY OF LIFE IS DEATH

The beauty of life is
certainty of death. I don't
fear death, I fear being alive…
yet not living. I am terrified
of wasting minutes that are mine,
the hours of this gift counting
away toward nothingness, no one
knowing how close to their end.

Death is the constant impetus to get
on with life, to experience what can be,
to love without fear, remembering this
breath one closer to your last.

Just one of you was ever made,
then gone forever, never again seeing,
never again feeling, never again knowing
warmth in love.

Death is inevitable, how I choose
to live decided the second
my eyes open. I choose to rage,
fighting until the last breath whispers
from my lips, moving towards what can
be, never regretting what was.

My life, an act of defiance, raging
against Death, who has never been beaten.
I am at peace with this inevitable storm,
knowing it will find me,
as it will find you.

SOON DEATH WHISPERED, SOON

Never thought about Death,
until he pulled up a stool next
to me at the bar.

Death gets bad press, always
the sulky guy wearing baggy
black robes, peeking from under
his hood, forever the grim reaper,
the rusty scythe of death in his
gnarled hand.

Death looked tired, eyes that have
witnessed an eternity of last minutes,
a working man patiently waiting
for next on the list, an overworked guy
in a never-ending job, never a day
without a life to end.

I should be dead. Raging drunken nights,
drugs, other men's women, all should
have killed me. But never the pleasure
of cocktails with Death, no last name
needed, never a chance to buy God's
hitman a drink or ask the purveyor
of last days how will I end?

I bought Death good whisky, on the rocks,
touch of spring water. His face ragged,
lines of sadness, tired of ones screaming,
begging for mercy when his strong hand
takes their last breath, crying for more time
in a life never lived.

I don't chase Death, but I keep him close, he
looking over my shoulder, a reminder to get on
with it, to savor the minutes, worship the hours,
dream of years never to be mine.

He rose to leave, whispered in my ear. *Not today friend, but soon, soon I will come for another whisky... and I will pay for the final round.*